EXPERIENCE THE CAPTIVATING JOURNEY OF ALEX IN "THE RISE OF THE FOOTBALL STAR: A CHAMPION IS BORN." FOLLOW THIS DETERMINED YOUNG BOY AS HE DEFIES THE ODDS, OVERCOMING CHALLENGES AND EMBRACING HIS PASSION FOR FOOTBALL. DISCOVER THE TRANSFORMATIVE POWER OF PERSEVERANCE AND WITNESS HOW SIZE BECOMES AN ADVANTAGE FOR THIS LITTLE BUT MIGHTY FOOTBALLER. GET READY TO BE INSPIRED AS ALEX'S STORY UNFOLDS, PROVING THAT GREATNESS KNOWS NO BOUNDARIES.

- Chapter 1: Alex's Love for Football — 1
- Chapter 2: Moving To a Bigger Club — 5
- Chapter 3: The First Game — 13
- Chapter 4: Little But Mighty Footballer — 19
- Chapter 5: The Big Game — 23
- Epilogue : Alex's Legacy — 31

CHAPTER 1: ALEX'S LOVE FOR FOOTBALL

Alex was a small boy who lived in a quiet town. He loved nothing more than playing football with his friends.

Every day, after school, he would rush to the park to kick the ball around. He dreamed of one day becoming a professional footballer, just like his heroes on TV.

Alex played for the local team, a small club that played on a tiny field at the edge of town.

It wasn't much, but it was where Alex's passion for football grew. He loved the feeling of the wind rushing past his face as he ran down the field, the sound of his feet hitting the grass, and the thrill of scoring a goal.

CHAPTER 1: ALEX'S LOVE FOR FOOTBALL

DESPITE HIS SMALL SIZE, ALEX WAS FEARLESS ON THE FIELD. HE WOULD GO UP AGAINST PLAYERS TWICE HIS SIZE AND NEVER BACK DOWN.

HE KNEW THAT IF HE WANTED TO BE A GREAT FOOTBALL PLAYER, HE HAD TO WORK HARD AND NEVER GIVE UP. HE KNEW THAT IF HE WORKED HARD ENOUGH, HE COULD ACHIEVE HIS DREAMS.

ALEX'S PARENTS WOULD OFTEN WATCH HIM PLAY, CHEERING HIM ON FROM THE SIDELINES.

THEY COULD SEE THE SPARK IN HIS EYE AND THE PASSION IN HIS HEART, AND THEY WERE PROUD OF THEIR LITTLE FOOTBALLER. LITTLE DID HE KNOW, THAT DREAM WAS CLOSER THAN HE THOUGHT...

CHAPTER 2 : MOVING TO A BIGGER CLUB

ONE DAY, ALEX'S LOCAL TEAM PLAYED A FRIENDLY MATCH AGAINST A LARGER CLUB FROM THE NEARBY CITY. ALEX PLAYED HIS HEART OUT AND CAUGHT THE EYE OF ONE OF THE SCOUTS FROM THE VISITING TEAM.

AFTER THE MATCH, THE SCOUT APPROACHED ALEX AND HIS PARENTS. "YOUR SON HAS A LOT OF TALENT," HE SAID. "WE WOULD LIKE TO INVITE HIM TO TRAIN WITH OUR TEAM AND SEE IF HE WOULD LIKE TO JOIN US."

ALEX WAS STUNNED. HE COULDN'T BELIEVE THAT A HILLFORD UNITED, MUCH BIGGER CLUB HAD NOTICED HIM, AND HE WAS BOTH EXCITED AND NERVOUS AT THE THOUGHT OF PLAYING FOR THEM.

ALEX NODDED, HIS HEART RACING WITH EXCITEMENT. HE KNEW THIS WAS HIS CHANCE TO MAKE HIS DREAMS COME TRUE.

CHAPTER 2 : MOVING TO A BIGGER CLUB

THE FOLLOWING WEEK, ALEX STARTED TRAINING WITH THE NEW TEAM.

HILLFORD UNITED!

HE WAS NERVOUS AT FIRST, BUT THE OTHER PLAYERS WELCOMED HIM WITH OPEN ARMS. ALEX QUICKLY REALIZED THAT HE HAD A LOT TO LEARN, BUT HE WAS DETERMINED TO WORK HARD AND IMPROVE.

THE NEW TEAM WAS MUCH BIGGER AND MORE PROFESSIONAL THAN ALEX'S OLD CLUB. THEY HAD A HUGE STADIUM AND SOME OF THE BEST COACHES IN THE COUNTRY. ALEX WAS IN AWE OF IT ALL.

BUT WITH THE EXCITEMENT CAME PRESSURE. ALEX KNEW THAT HE HAD TO PROVE HIMSELF IF HE WANTED TO STAY WITH THE TEAM. HE TRAINED HARDER THAN EVER BEFORE, PRACTICING EVERY DAY AND WORKING ON HIS SKILLS.

CHAPTER 2 : MOVING TO A BIGGER CLUB

AFTER SEVERAL WEEKS OF HARD WORK, ALEX FINALLY GOT HIS CHANCE. THE COACH CALLED HIM UP TO PLAY IN A FRIENDLY MATCH AGAINST ANOTHER BIG CLUB. ALEX WAS NERVOUS, BUT HE KNEW HE HAD TO GIVE IT HIS ALL.

AND THAT'S EXACTLY WHAT HE DID. ALEX PLAYED HIS HEART OUT, SHOWING OFF ALL THE SKILLS HE HAD LEARNED DURING HIS TIME WITH THE NEW TEAM. AT THE END OF THE MATCH, THE COACH PRAISED ALEX'S PERFORMANCE AND TOLD HIM HE WAS OFFICIALLY ON THE TEAM.

ALEX COULDN'T BELIEVE IT. HE HAD WORKED SO HARD FOR THIS MOMENT, AND IT HAD FINALLY PAID OFF. HE WAS NOW A PART OF A BIGGER CLUB, WITH BIGGER GOALS AND BIGGER DREAMS. AND HE WAS READY TO MAKE THEM ALL COME TRUE.

CHAPTER 3: THE FIRST GAME

ALEX WAS THRILLED TO BE PART OF THE BIGGER CLUB, BUT HE KNEW THAT IT CAME WITH NEW CHALLENGES. HE HAD TO WORK EVEN HARDER TO KEEP UP WITH THE OTHER PLAYERS AND EARN HIS SPOT ON THE TEAM. HE COULDN'T WAIT TO PLAY HIS FIRST GAME.

AS THE GAME BEGAN, ALEX FELT NERVOUS BUT EXCITED. HE WAS DETERMINED TO SHOW HIS TEAMMATES AND COACHES WHAT HE WAS CAPABLE OF.

BUT AS THE GAME WENT ON, ALEX REALIZED THAT PLAYING WITH A BIGGER TEAM WAS A LOT HARDER THAN PLAYING IN THE SMALL CLUB. HE STRUGGLED TO KEEP UP WITH THE OTHER PLAYERS AND FOUND IT HARD TO GET THE BALL.

AT TIMES, HE FELT LIKE HE WAS INVISIBLE, LIKE NO ONE WAS PASSING THE BALL TO HIM.

CHAPTER 3: THE FIRST GAME

BUT EVEN AS HE STRUGGLED, ALEX REFUSED TO GIVE UP. HE KEPT RUNNING UP AND DOWN THE FIELD, TRYING TO GET THE BALL AND MAKE A PLAY.

AND THEN, IN THE SECOND HALF OF THE GAME, ALEX GOT HIS CHANCE. ONE OF HIS TEAMMATES PASSED HIM THE BALL, AND ALEX RAN WITH IT, DODGING THE OPPOSING TEAM'S DEFENDERS AND

SCORING A GOAL!!!

THE TEAM ERUPTED IN CHEERS, AND ALEX FELT A SURGE OF PRIDE AND JOY. HE REALIZED THAT EVEN THOUGH HE WAS SMALL, HE COULD STILL MAKE A BIG IMPACT ON THE GAME.

FROM THAT MOMENT ON, ALEX FELT MORE CONFIDENT ON THE FIELD, KNOWING THAT HE HAD THE SUPPORT OF HIS TEAM AND THE ABILITY TO MAKE A DIFFERENCE.

CHAPTER 4: LITTLE BUT MIGHTY FOOTBALLER

AS ALEX CONTINUED TO PLAY WITH HIS TEAM, HE BEGAN TO REALIZE THAT HE STILL HAD A LOT TO LEARN ABOUT THE GAME. HE LOVED PLAYING FOOTBALL, BUT HE KNEW THAT HE NEEDED TO WORK ON HIS SKILLS TO BECOME A BETTER PLAYER.

ONE DAY, AS ALEX WAS PRACTICING ON HIS OWN, AN OLDER FOOTBALL PLAYER APPROACHED HIM. THE PLAYER HAD NOTICED ALEX'S SMALL SIZE BUT WAS IMPRESSED WITH HIS DETERMINATION ON THE FIELD.

THE PLAYER INTRODUCED HIMSELF AS COACH MIKE AND OFFERED TO GIVE ALEX SOME ADVICE ABOUT PERSEVERANCE, TEAMWORK AND MINDSET.

ALEX LISTENED INTENTLY TO COACH MIKE'S ADVICE AND REALIZED THAT HE TOO COULD BECOME A BETTER PLAYER IF HE PERSEVERED AND WORKED ON HIS SKILLS.

CHAPTER 4: LITTLE BUT MIGHTY FOOTBALLER

AS A FINAL PIECE OF ADVICE, COACH MIKE SAID: "NEVER UNDERESTIMATE THE IMPACT OF A POSITIVE MINDSET. YOUR HEIGHT DOESN'T DEFINE YOUR POTENTIAL AS A FOOTBALL PLAYER. EMBRACE YOUR UNIQUE ATTRIBUTES, WORK HARD, AND ENJOY THE GAME TO THE FULLEST."

HE DECIDED TO EMBRACE HIS SMALL SIZE AND USE IT TO HIS ADVANTAGE. HE FOCUSED ON HIS SPEED AND AGILITY, USING HIS SMALL FRAME TO DODGE PAST DEFENDERS AND MAKE PLAYS.

AS THE SEASON WENT ON, ALEX'S SKILLS IMPROVED. HE ALSO BECAME A KEY MEMBER OF HIS TEAM, WITH HIS TEAMMATES RELYING ON HIM TO SCORE GOALS.

AND AS HE LOOKED BACK ON HIS JOURNEY, ALEX REALIZED THAT HIS SMALL SIZE HAD NEVER HELD HIM BACK. INSTEAD, IT HAD BEEN HIS DETERMINATION AND HARD WORK THAT HAD LED HIM TO BECOME THE LITTLE BUT MIGHTY FOOTBALLER THAT HE WAS TODAY.

CHAPTER 5: THE BIG GAME

ALEX'S TEAM WON GAME AFTER GAME, AND THEY EVENTUALLY MADE IT TO THE CHAMPIONSHIP MATCH. THIS WAS THE BIGGEST GAME OF THE YEAR, AND EVERYONE WAS NERVOUS.

THE DAY OF THE CHAMPIONSHIP MATCH ARRIVED, AND THE STADIUM WAS PACKED WITH FANS. ALEX'S TEAM WAS UP AGAINST A TOUGH OPPONENT, BUT THEY WERE READY TO FIGHT.

THE GAME WAS INTENSE, WITH BOTH TEAMS PLAYING THEIR HEARTS OUT. THE SCORE WAS TIED, AND THERE WERE ONLY A FEW MINUTES LEFT ON THE CLOCK.

SUDDENLY, ALEX SAW HIS CHANCE. THE BALL WAS COMING TOWARDS HIM, AND HE KNEW THAT HE HAD TO MAKE A PLAY.

WITH HIS HEART POUNDING, ALEX RACED TOWARDS THE BALL, DODGING PAST DEFENDERS WITH EASE. HE COULD HEAR HIS TEAMMATES SHOUTING HIS NAME, URGING HIM ON.

CHAPTER 5: THE BIG GAME

WITH ONE SWIFT KICK, ALEX SENT THE BALL FLYING TOWARDS THE GOAL. THE CROWD HELD THEIR BREATH AS THE BALL SAILED THROUGH THE AIR, AND THEN...

GOAL!!!

THE STADIUM ERUPTED IN CHEERS AS ALEX'S TEAM SCORED THE WINNING GOAL.

ALEX WAS OVERJOYED. HE HAD NEVER FELT SO PROUD OF HIMSELF AND HIS TEAM.

AS THE TEAM CELEBRATED THEIR VICTORY, ALEX KNEW THAT HE HAD BECOME A TRUE FOOTBALL CHAMPION. HE HAD PROVEN THAT SIZE DIDN'T MATTER, AND THAT WITH HEART AND DETERMINATION, ANYTHING WAS POSSIBLE.

CHAPTER 5: THE BIG GAME

AFTER THE MATCH, ALEX WAS SURROUNDED BY FANS AND REPORTERS, ALL EAGER TO TALK TO THE YOUNG FOOTBALLER WHO HAD BECOME A CHAMPION. ALEX WAS OVERWHELMED, BUT HE SMILED AND ANSWERED ALL OF THEIR QUESTIONS, GRATEFUL FOR THE OPPORTUNITY TO SHARE HIS STORY.

THE STORY OF THE SMALL FOOTBALLER WHO STARTED IN A SMALL CLUB, BUT THROUGH HIS PERSEVERANCE AND DETERMINATION, HE HAD BECOME A CHAMPION. AND HE HOPED THAT HIS STORY WOULD INSPIRE OTHER YOUNG FOOTBALLERS TO FOLLOW THEIR DREAMS, NO MATTER HOW BIG OR SMALL THEY MIGHT SEEM.

EPILOGUE: ALEX'S LEGACY

ALEX'S JOURNEY HAD BEEN A CHALLENGING ONE, BUT IT HAD TAUGHT HIM MANY IMPORTANT LESSONS. HE HAD LEARNED THE VALUE OF TEAMWORK, PERSEVERANCE, AND BELIEVING IN ONESELF.

ALEX'S STORY WAS AN INSPIRATION TO MANY, AND HIS LEGACY LIVED ON. HE HAD BECOME KNOWN AS THE LITTLE BUT MIGHTY FOOTBALLER, A PLAYER WHO HAD DEFIED THE ODDS AND ACHIEVED GREATNESS THROUGH HARD WORK AND DETERMINATION.

ALEX HOPED THAT HIS STORY WOULD ENCOURAGE OTHERS TO PURSUE THEIR PASSIONS AND NEVER GIVE UP ON THEIR DREAMS. HE WANTED TO SHOW THAT ANYTHING WAS POSSIBLE, NO MATTER HOW BIG OR SMALL ONE MIGHT BE.

EPILOGUE: ALEX'S LEGACY

AND ALEX HAD ALSO BECOME A MENTOR, TAKING YOUNG FOOTBALLERS UNDER HIS WING AND SHARING HIS KNOWLEDGE AND EXPERIENCE WITH THEM. HE HAD BECOME A ROLE MODEL, NOT JUST FOR HIS SKILLS ON THE FIELD, BUT FOR HIS CHARACTER OFF IT.

AND AS HE LOOKED BACK ON HIS JOURNEY, ALEX KNEW THAT HE HAD LEFT A SMALL BUT MIGHTY LEGACY, ONE THAT WOULD INSPIRE OTHERS TO BELIEVE IN THEMSELVES AND REACH FOR THE STARS.

Printed in Great Britain
by Amazon